MW01248138

Wholeheartedly

Wholeheartedly

A COLLECTIVE WORK OF SISTERHOOD

MYND
MATTERS

Copyright © 2024

All rights reserved. No part of this publication may be reproduced, distributed, or transmitted in any form or by any means, including photocopying, recording, or other electronic or mechanical methods, without the prior written permission of the publisher, except in the case of brief quotations embodied in critical reviews and certain other noncommercial uses permitted by copyright law. If you would like permission to use material from the book (other than for review purposes), please contact the publisher.

Thank you for your support of the author's rights.

Books may be purchased in bulk quantity and/or special sales by contacting the publisher.

Published by Mynd Matters Publishing
www.myndmatterspublishing.com

978-1-957092-99-7 (pbk)
978-1-963874-00-6 (hdc)
978-1-963874-01-3 (ebk)

FIRST EDITION

Contents

Introduction

The courage and call of one woman to unite nine amazing souls for one weekend of soul rejuvenation in Mt. Croghan, South Carolina, has created a sister bond of support and joy and a movement of global impact.

Vallori Thomas, Life Coach, author, and visionary, enrolled women from all walks of life to commune with nature, one another, and themselves for relaxation and an opportunity to get light. It was true servant-leadership in operation. We had a time, and we'll never be the same.

Hailing from Pennsylvania through Florida, we are a diverse group: single, married, divorced, and widowed. Some are nurturers of our own children and all are caregivers and protectors of the community. We have careers as nurses, beauticians, social activists, healers, federal government workers—you name it. These ten talents were loosed to produce a ripple effect of growth, inclusion, and possibility by simply living and sharing their amazing gifts and holding one another up to our highest. Unique and complete in our own beings, we offer ourselves *wholeheartedly*.

CHAPTER 1

Taundrea Tavada

Fear, Gratitude & Evolving

I am a young woman with brown skin approaching her 50s. I am educated with a degree in engineering, working in construction. I am a people person. I go to the park to watch people walk around, always observing. I found my voice several years ago and have been manifesting a way to be heard. *What do I do with this voice? Does anybody care about what I say? Is what I say valuable?*

Through reflection and prayer, I claimed that my perspective matters! I am an authentic, passionate, trusting woman. Once I landed in this space in my head, I have been discovering myself. This weekend, I'm really going to be put to the test. I enlisted a new girlfriend, Tia, which I never do, to come with me on the trip to the middle of nowhere, South Carolina.

She's been struggling with some things in her life and I think this trip will open some things for her and for myself. Ironically, it takes place right near her property which was recently burned to the ground.

I was excited and nervous. When you do the work, it requires peeling back layers that aren't as comfortable as you thought they would be. There is strength in breaking down or at least being able to try. That's what we're up against—the willingness to grow.

I wrapped up everything at work and prepared to make the four-hour drive to nowhere. I had my music lined up. Some gospel and a special playlist created by Vallori, my coach. My phone was charged, and I packed everything I would need.

The initial part of the drive was filled with reminiscing about how many times I had been to this place I called "the middle of nowhere," what I'd gotten from it, and why I recalled going and not knowing what I was going into. The only information I had was that it would be made up of a group of women who I assumed were amazing, authentic, and dealing with a lot of the same issues I was dealing with. There are a few people in my life that can ask of me and I will blindly go. Vallori is one of them.

As it turned out, these wonderful ladies allowed me to discover and see myself in a lot of different ways. I experienced Reiki for the first time, and my energy resonated with the trees and the lake. Oh, and the dog, Rocky—he was wonderful. He became my new companion while walking the grounds. He walked with me everywhere I wanted to go and reminded me of my dog growing up. He was protective and therefore, always by my side.

There were two other times I attended this place, and each time I learned something new about myself. I forgave myself a little more about things I struggled with in the past. I hoped my girlfriend would experience some of the same things during our weekend. I was really excited she decided to come.

She's one of my good girlfriends. She's been ride or die with me every day for a year and a half, although we have been friends since college. I had been going through a rough journey over the last two years and was hoping I could offer something to her that would be of some use as she had often been to me.

The second half of the trip involved more talking to Tia on the phone and easing her fears about going into a situation with a bunch of strange women. I told her I thought it was gonna be one of the best weekends ever. See, as women, we struggle with parenting, being good professionals, being a good girlfriend or wife, and remembering to take care of ourselves. We forget to take time to check in. This is what I use as my check-in. I went there that weekend to check in with myself, to release some things, and to also pick up some good tools to manage the rest of the journey. That's what I went to receive. I thought, *I wonder what I have to give, though.*

Questions and thoughts bounced around in my head. *What am I bringing to the table?* I'm bringing my whole self. I'm bringing myself in the middle of a journey that I don't even know where it ends. I hoped to identify more of that while there but I figured I was at a good starting point. I just knew whoever was in the room was there to receive, to give, and to learn from.

I only had about an hour left when the drive became dark. *These roads are really, really dark. It's almost like traversing in my brain sometimes.* Fighting the darkness can be tough when you don't know where you're going. You don't know where your support is, and you're not even sure if there is support. I started thinking about trust. *Do I trust myself? Do I trust these people?* What I've come to realize is I only have to trust the Lord, and that's not even a "have to." That's a choice.

Tia and I arrived at the same time. I believed we were the last ones to arrive as we pulled up. It was nice to see Tia, and I felt safe knowing she was there. As we entered the gate in our separate cars, I felt the energy. It was almost overwhelming. As we were driving down the long path to get to the house, I felt a big hug. One I didn't expect but needed.

We got out of our cars, hugged, and laughed as we prepared to walk into the main house where the other ladies were already meeting. *I'm really hungry. I hope they plan to cook.*

I couldn't wait to see what this weekend released and healed in me. They had already begun eating while the coach spoke to the group. I was starving, but also observant. I saw these beautiful ladies and was aware of the energy in the room. It was very nervous and tense, which was a bit unexpected. Tia and I sat down, and our plates, a bountiful selection of veggies, fish, and rice, were served. The conversation was about being intentional and knowing that this group of women tends to check out. Now that hit me hard. I know I do it…can't wait to see how they do it. The energy in the room was excited, yet hesitant, but also open. There were nine ladies total, plus a coach. *This is going to be an amazing weekend.*

My thoughts were everywhere as we finished our first dinner. I wondered what these ladies' stories were and how I would relate to them. Tia and I were soaking everything in. The house was absolutely beautiful. I missed the familiar sense of peace, strength, and love. It so thickly encompassed my heart. I took a deep breath and an intentional look around. The walls were earth tones of burnt orange and contrasting brighter hues of a mix of tangerine and clementine. The sculptures all had their own energy.

There were two women I was totally fond of because their breasts were perky and full, and their lips were full. They looked like sisters I could've had. They exuded the strength and presence of a woman. There was also a man crouched over, sitting cross-legged with his head down. I rubbed his back, and the touch gave me a moment of sadness. It felt as though this man had been through it all and found this position as his peace. My journey has also felt like an endless struggle at times. As I embraced my atmosphere, I realized there was an aroma of love in the air. I couldn't quite explain it, but if I were to try, it would be a sweet vanilla chocolate smell with a mix of lavender and a hint of cinnamon. It felt cuddly yet resolved. Like a hug from my grandma on a Sunday afternoon out of the blue. *I feel safe.* After brief introductions and some laughter, we all headed to our sleeping quarters. As we got settled in our rooms, conversations took place in small groups.

We had one kickoff session that night back at the main house with Coach Vallori. Nine ladies gathered in the meditation room for our kickoff session, and I was bit nervous. I had my usual "am I good enough to be here" talk in my head. All the ladies looked so put together and distinguished. I was intimidated but also intrigued because maybe those qualities could brush off on me. But how do I know what they bring to the table? *They may be just as out of sorts as I am.*

I shook off the negative self-talk and observed the ladies before the session began. There was one woman who looked like my cousin. The cousin with the big energy. *I wonder if she is the same.* Another looked like she was mad or holding something that might get taken away. *I wonder what she's holding.* I recognized that look because I have it when I am among strangers. It's the untaught way of a northern city girl who must use her expressions for protection in the streets. *I wonder where she's from.* I also checked for Tia to make sure she was alright, and she looked back with assurance.

Vallori joined us and started the session. Her initial statements were clear and intriguing.

"The reason I picked you ladies is because we all have a way of disappearing."

When the words hit my ears and travelled through my brain and dropped into my heart, I felt a moment of sadness. This was a feeling I usually didn't allow to surface. The feeling that I didn't matter because when I disappear, no one comes checking for me. From family to friends, I recalled the times when I pulled away remaining lonely and disappointed. When I wanted someone to notice or see me—and in my absence, they did not. I hold that pain deep.

With her statement, she also reminded me that others may experience the same thing and react the same way by disappearing. Instantly the word "reflection" popped into my head. *These ladies are reflections of me!*

The session was very powerful in that each of us had a moment to share who we are, how we are feeling, and how we got to be in the middle of nowhere. As I listened, I connected to each woman in so many ways. Each connection peeled a layer of my soul back, safely revealing some uncomfortable pains. *I know why I am here. I am so grateful.* As I convinced my heart to release, I also began to absorb the love energy from the ladies.

Never underestimate the wonderful feeling of a deep breath and the release that takes place. It's powerful! As we walked back to the cabin on the first night, my soul was healing, and peace was moving through me. As I opened the door and entered the cabin, I looked over at the door of my room for the weekend and it read, "GRATITUDE." *Ahh, this is exactly where I need to be!*

The rest of the weekend was powerful and filled with exercises and tools to release and restore. We all became closer through sharing our experiences and lots of laughter. The more we released, the more we restored. I had a massage and participated in a Reiki session. Prior to attending, I had been introduced to energy and discovered different studies around it, so I was excited to have my session. Karina, the Reiki practitioner, and I began our hour-long session in the early afternoon. During the session, there was a point when the area she was focused on became hot.

Karina said, "Is there something going on that makes you feel stuck or stagnant?"

I began to recall many times when I tried to be something, and it failed. I began to see the points in my life when I did not feel good enough or that I belonged. The sadness seemed to manifest in this hot spot, and it grew hotter.

"These thoughts, do they have a person that stands out?" Karina asked.

I was quiet but then, like watching a movie, I saw an image of my mom staring back at me.

"My mom."

"Tell me about her."

I expressed to Karina that I had felt love from my mom, a great love. And I felt I was love since I was born on Valentine's Day as a love gift to my mom. As I stared into my mom's face, I could feel her love energy, and my chest became warm. It felt like when you drink a hot beverage on a really cold day, and the warmth flows from your mouth down into your chest.

As the memories of feeling not good enough started to compete with the now flashes of my mom's face, I began to forgive her. I began to see her flaws in love as a woman who loves a human who loves. And then I began to see and feel my love for my children. I saw their faces and their tears, and the energy took over my body as it began to tremble with Karina focused now on my chest.

"Let it go and be free," she said in a soft but assertive gentle voice. "Forgive yourself and love yourself." This time her voice was almost a whisper.

My thoughts came up. *Girl, you know you made some jacked-up decisions. Girl, you know you knew better when you chose that thing.*

And then Karina said, "You know who you are. You are love."

Silence and stillness came over me.

"You're a tough cookie," said Karina.

I took a deep breath and smiled. As I walked out of our session, a gentle whisper said, *Love is patient. Love is kind…*

The remainder of the weekend was a process of embracing the space left from releasing those pains and basking in forgiveness along with a lot of laughter. We all ate good, laughed plenty, and shared our lives—the struggles, joys, and praises. We communed and vibrated on a high level. We meditated every morning allowing the soul to prepare to embrace the new discoveries of everyday.

On the final day in the meditation for that morning, I became overwhelmed in gratitude to tears. My mind and my heart sang a song of peace while my thoughts were rehashing all the joy from my overall experience as a human—on that day, in that moment. The experience was like a big dance. I danced with each one of the women, entertained in the details shared along with the energy. The playlist was the song of each of our hearts, creating a vibration that rang the earth like a bell. Tia and I embraced before getting into our respective cars to leave. It was an embrace that required no words! I am so grateful for my life and my journey as I continue to discover me!

Questions for the Reader:

1. What is your process of discovering more of you?

2. How can you find gratitude in your journey?

CHAPTER 2

Evelyn White

The Strength
I Never Knew I Had

Thanking God every day for preparing me for what He has prepared for me. Things don't happen to us, they happen *for* us. I was my mother's tenth child and the only girl. Having me meant her wish had finally come true. My mother had high hopes and dreams for a little girl but had no clue how to take care of her because she'd only had boys, and out of the nine, only three survived.

As my mom lived, a promising career as an actor meant little time for the children. As she struggled with balancing acting, partying, and parenting, my grandmother and uncles stepped in to assist. When I was about five or six, I lived with my nana and her husband in upstate New York. I lived for the weekends because that's when we would go down to visit my mom and brothers.

My grandmother was that woman who was highly respected and ran card games from Friday to Sunday. Know for sure that all gamblers had to pay the house which was my Nana. From early on, I knew my Nana carried a pistol in her purse and under her pillow and was never afraid to use it.

When I was around seven or eight, I no longer liked my weekend trips to leave my mother, especially when Nana had to stay in the city. As a child, I didn't understand when my grandfather, aka Dad, would come into my room late at night. He would massage my body, especially between my legs. He would always say this is our little secret and that I can't tell anyone. For my keeping our secret, I would receive various gifts, especially for the holidays.

As time moved forward and a couple of years passed, we moved down south. I joined track and field as an outlet to escape what was going on at night when my Nana was away for her business trips. I was old enough to know that what was happening to me was about to be happening to my cousin. No one believed her until I said she was not lying. It had been happening to me for years. The question my aunts and uncle wanted to know was, "Why did I never say anything."

Here's where the strength I never had kicked in. I told them I never said anything because I knew Nana had a pistol in her purse, and she, Mommy, or my uncle would kill him. If they went to jail, who would raise me? I didn't realize that this was where my way of concealing started.

By the time I reached fifteen, all the seeds my Nana poured and planted in me started to manifest. My uncle moved us from around my grandfather. I was able to confront him and tell him what he was doing to me was wrong and that it stopped that day. He apologized, but in the next breath, and because my Nana was really sick, he said that's a need he had. I stood up to my grandfather with such conviction and told him if he dared touch me again, everyone in the family would know. With my Nana having terminal cancer at the time, it made me realize that she'd worked so hard for me to have a better life. Right after we moved down south and with Nana being in politics, she had a Community Center built for the youth and seniors. Through the curriculum, it provided me with the foundational skills I would need in life. I was able to use my own experiences to help young people who may also be suffering.

I used to ask God why He let this happen to me. I

knew it wasn't love. I now see that I can use my Strength and be a voice for those who don't have the words but know they are being mistreated and hurt. I can be the change for other children who are experiencing molestation and abuse silently. God equipped me with all the tools I needed, especially the strength I didn't know I had.

Questions for the Reader:

1. Innocence is a strength that we don't often know we have. Can you identify a personal strength you didn't know you had?

2. How do you continue to build that personal strength muscle? Who/what can support you in this?

CHAPTER 3

Ana Moncion Dominguez

The Desert

Dedicated to my beloved mother, Gloria Castro (April 1, 1946 – March 9, 2022). Not everyone gets to experience the kind of love she bestowed upon me.

Metaphorically, the desert is a place of testing and transformation—of being divested of empire or ego. In the desert experience, the dreams, goals, and visions of the false self can be seen clearly. Sometimes for the first time. The desert signifies the terrain where we unlearn and undo.

"He found him in a desert land, in the waste howling wilderness. He surrounded him. He cared for him. He kept him as the apple of His eye." (Deuteronomy 32:10)

I got locked up abroad. It all happened so fast. My

husband was in jail. I met this great-looking Colombian guy at the club. We hung out and partied a few times. At the time, I was struggling to pay my bills. My rent was backed up, the lights were about to be cut off, and all the other bills kept mounting. I was enrolled in college, and tuition was due. I reached out to my Colombian "friend" Marcos. Colombians were known to be in the drug game, so, I asked if he knew of anyone who needed a courier or a stash house. He said he'd get back to me. The next day he called to say his contact needed a courier to transport eleven kilos of cocaine from Panama to New York. He said it would be so easy. He also told me they have a team of women who brought merchandise weekly, but one of them was sick, and suddenly, there was a slot available for me. The pay was $50,000.

Next thing I know, I'm on a plane to Panama. I left my nine-year-old daughter at my aunt's house. I lied and said I was going for a job interview with American Airlines at their corporate offices in Texas. I promised to be back in three days. On the plane ride, all I could think about was the $50,000. At twenty-eight years old, I had never even dreamed of that much money, much less having it in my hands. Marco had paid for the flight and hotel and gave me a $2,000 cash advance. Then, I was on my way.

My arrival in Panama was not a good experience. The officials greeted me with disdain and borderline disrespect. They kept asking why I was there, what I was going to do while there, who I was going to see, who sent me, and where I was staying. Marco had already warned me that they would ask a lot of questions because it was my first time there.

When I arrived at the hotel, it was actually a cheap motel in the worst-looking neighborhood. It looked like a whore house. The room was the size of a broom closet, and there was one disgusting bathroom to be shared by everyone on that floor. No way was I going to stay there. I asked the receptionist what the best hotel in the city was, and he told me the Hotel Panama. I grabbed my suitcase, jumped in a cab, and told the driver, "Hotel Panama, por favor."

Once I checked in, I was content. The room was spacious and clean, and I had my own bathroom. It was overlooking the pool and had a great view of the city. I called Marco and told him I moved to a different hotel. He asked for my room number and said someone would contact me.

Panama City was vibrant and festive. Carnival was in full swing, and the streets were alive with music. People wore colorful and elaborate costumes. The parade was right outside my hotel window. I went outside and I was swept away by the vibes. The street food was succulent, the men were gorgeous, and the women were beautiful. The sound of the drums beat all the way into my heart and soul. I ate, I danced, I laughed. Oh, what a night!

The next day, the man came to see me. He explained that the merchandise would arrive later that day in boxes inside of electronic equipment. I stayed in the hotel room all day—the two boxes arrived in the evening. My flight back to New York was at 10 a.m. the following day. That night, I dreamed I got arrested. When I woke up, I was uneasy. I knew deep in my gut something was not right. I dismissed those thoughts and feelings. I lied to myself by not touching the boxes, so my fingerprints would be nowhere on them. I called reception and had the bellboy bring down the two boxes along with my luggage.

When I arrived at the airport, the taxi driver loaded the boxes and my suitcase onto the belt. One of the airline workers asked out loud, "Who do these boxes belong to? They must go through the machine again."

I picked up my suitcase and walked away. I got in the line to present my ticket and passport. *Fuck it—I'm just gonna leave those boxes. I'm not getting arrested.* I was next in line when I got tapped on the shoulder by an airport employee. He was accompanied by a police officer. He asked to see my passport, took it out of my hands, and said, "Please accompany me."

They took me to a room. The officer explained that the airport security cameras clearly showed me getting out of a cab with the two boxes. They broke open the boxes and pulled out twenty-two kilos of pure cocaine. *Not 11?!*

There were a lot of officers coming in and out of the room. I got fingerprinted, photographed, and they read me my rights. I chose to stay silent. I was handcuffed and taken to the women's prison, Centro Femenino de Rehabilitacion (CFR). Up until that moment, I was in a trance. I was so calm that one of the officers commented on how relaxed I was for a person who was in such dire circumstances. He said I could be facing twenty plus years in prison for trafficking that amount of drugs. I gave him a blank stare.

I was escorted to a small dark, musty, and HOT cell. The door slammed HARD behind me. There were more than a dozen women lying on the floor, leaning on the walls or standing up. They all just stared at me. Someone made a little space for me. As I leaned against the wall and slid my ass to the floor, the reality of the situation slammed me like a tidal wave. I was drowning, I couldn't breathe.

Oh my God! MY DAUGHTER, MY MOM, MY

DAD, MY BROTHERS, MY HUSBAND, MY FAMILY, MY FRIENDS. No one knew where I was or what was happening to me. I was ashamed, embarrassed, scared, terrified, and all alone in jail in a foreign country. I cried until I had no more tears. I didn't eat or drink anything. I don't know how, but I fell into a deep sleep. I was startled out of my sleep by the sound of the door slamming. I was escorted out of the cell to what looked like a conference room. The woman identified herself as a social worker. She allowed me to make a phone call, and I called my brother. My darling brother was so loving and supportive during the call. He told me not to worry, and that I was not alone. He told me they were going to get me out of there.

The next day, a lawyer showed up. He said he had been hired by my family. The first thing he did was move me out of the holding cell. I was moved to the main prison, where I was assigned to live in a "house" with forty-nine other women—twenty-five bunk beds, three shower stalls, and two toilets. There were murderers, prostitutes, drug dealers, thieves, illegal immigrants, and then there was me…the mule. Aside from their legal status and the crimes they had committed, they were mostly good women who had been caught up in a bad situation, just like me.

It took one year for my case to be tried in court. I

was in a desert. During that year, I was tested and transformed. I was faced head-on with the reality of death. Silvie died of a heart attack, Tita had a stillbirth, and Rosario died of an asthma attack with an empty asthma pump in her hands. I was divested of my home, my family, my ego. All those dreams and goals of my "false self" came to light. For the first time, I found myself walking in this terrain, naked and alone, unlearning and undoing all the things I thought I knew to be true.

I read the Bible from beginning to end, and from the end to the beginning. I was allowed to leave the "house" and walk around the property unescorted, and my feet always led me to the little church. I attended mass every Sunday, and I encouraged my roommates to come and listen to the Word. One day, a ninety-year-old man showed up at the prison to volunteer his services. He was a musician, and he set up a band so we could play the music at church. I played the guitar, Tita played the recorder, Penny played the drums, and we had five singers with angelic voices. Sunday service was amazing.

I've always been an avid reader. I had already read every book that everyone owned in the place. The ambassador came to visit all American citizens monthly. She asked if we needed anything, and I replied, "We need sanitary napkins for our monthly flow, and we need books."

The next day, a truck from the United States embassy came with crates of maxi pads and hundreds of books. I shared the pads with all of the women. I read all the books. Eventually, my court day came. Everything happened fast. I was sentenced to ten years! The MAN said ten years, but GOD said four years.

After four years I was released. It was the spring of 1999. I'd learned my lesson. Since my release, I have never gotten into legal trouble again. My time in the desert was beneficial and necessary for me to become the mother, daughter, wife, sister, and friend I am today.

Today, I live in a state of gratitude and abundance. I've traveled the world. I've been at the same job for eighteen years, and this year I celebrated thirty-eight years of marriage. My brothers and I are more loving and connected than ever. My daughter graduated from college and is happily independent and thriving. The time had come to unlearn and undo.

Know that this is your strength!

Questions for the Reader

1. Many of us have had a desert experience where we thought or felt separated and alone based on a decision or act. Then, we realized there is something greater. What or who did you discover?

2. How has what you discovered challenged or shaped you?

CHAPTER 4

Kimberly Givens

The Act and Art of Kindness

I always say, "It's a privilege to have access to me." There are people who act like they want to be in your circle but, in fact, show up very differently. I wonder if you know what I mean.

If you've ever felt betrayed by someone you thought was your friend, and then realized this person could never be who you thought they were, could you be cordial and kind to them? Honestly, would you? It's important to keep in mind that their behavior is a reflection of them, not YOU. What's also important to remember is that being kind doesn't mean tolerating disrespectful or abusive behavior.

A friend I've known for over forty years betrayed me. Like a dagger to my heart, it hurt me deeply. I just never imagined someone I loved and trusted would treat me so differently or any less than I treated them. I never really got over it. Life and time went on, but that moment never left me…and neither did she. As time went on, I noticed a series of upsets and unwarranted conversations that somehow involved me, members of my family, and the people I worked with that I literally had no clue about. Wait…did I mention I married her brother? When someone is unkind to you, it can be quick and easy to draw conclusions, react, and feel. I waited several months before I said or did anything. First, because I am not confrontational and second, I loved her and really wanted to understand why. True talk, she never apologized or acknowledged what she said, what she did, or that she hurt my feelings or caused any upset. I realized I had to "let go of having to be right about how she was supposed to be and defend me." We have little control over other people's experiences. Forgive yourself for thinking otherwise. Their experiences are theirs. It's how they are wired, and the stories they create that unfold and form their lives.

Kindness is not about how others treat you, but about how you choose to treat others. Have you ever had an encounter with someone who wasn't nice and expected you to be kind to them anyway? They were belligerent, yet expected you not to react to their actions or words. A woman I worked with for eleven years had her own business. For some odd reason, she accused me of not "articulating" or "responding" the way she thought I should when it came to offering the location of her business to clients that we both knew. We had worked together for eleven years without any incidents. I couldn't believe her accusations. She went as far as to verbally attack me online via text and phone messaging. Can you imagine? I got a hold of myself and kindly addressed her. I offered that if she wanted to have lunch and talk about it, we could, but her accusations were false. Enough was enough! Remember, being kind is a choice you make, regardless of how others treat you. It is when we experience an action that is uncomfortable, that we begin to dissolve the ability to be kind. Ego is a big part of who we are and how we react. In our core, we are love and joy.

THE ART OF KINDNESS
Take nothing personal (this requires earnest practice).

Think of ways communication can be effective for you and them, and…stay there. Don't look for what used to be (presumptions). Look for the possibility. If that isn't possible, it's okay. Take note of what the lesson is or was, and "keep it movin'. Let go of having to be right about how they're supposed to behave.

By responding with empathy, kindness, and understanding, you can help create a more positive and compassionate environment, even in challenging situations. Be the example.

THE ACT OF KINDNESS

Acts of kindness can lead to positive emotions such as joy, gratitude, and contentment, both for the person who is being kind and the person who receives the kindness. Studies have shown that people who engage in regular acts of kindness tend to be happier and experience less stress and anxiety. When you are kind to someone, it can inspire them to be kind to others. This creates a ripple effect, where kindness spreads from person to person, leading to a more positive and compassionate society.

Overall, being kind is important because it not only benefits others, but it also benefits you. It promotes positive relationships, increases happiness, promotes empathy and compassion, and creates a positive ripple effect.

RESULTS OF KINDNESS

Acts of kindness can lead to positive emotions such as joy, gratitude, and contentment, both for the person who is being kind and the person who receives the kindness.

Questions for the Reader

1. If you felt betrayed by someone you thought was your friend and now realize this person could never be who you thought they were, could you be cordial and kind to this person? If so, how were you able to?

2. Being kind is who you are. Although you're angry with someone's decision that has affected you, how will you handle your interactions with this person now?

3. What is a kind thing you can do for someone today?

CHAPTER 5

Tracia Walters

It Hurts More to Leave Than to Stay

Many of us find ourselves in situations we didn't see coming. For some years I was in a relationship with someone I trusted. It was always just something about this person that I couldn't shake. I saw more in this person than he saw in himself. There was something about our relationship that was different than any other relationship I've had in my life. During the course of the relationship, I discovered the things I wanted and the things I did not want. Looking back at that time, I have no regrets. It's clear to me everything happens for a reason.

One day while having a conversation with a friend of mine, she revealed some information about the person I was in a relationship with. The shit CRUSHED me! See, the thing is, I knew, but I was in denial. I remember crying and having an ache in my heart. I called my pastor and sat on the phone crying, unable to get the words out. It was a cry of hurt. The pastor prayed and prayed, and told me I was going to be fine. "God's got you, and you got this."

As a woman going through situations like this, your friends and family will typically advise you to leave. Many will have the worst to say about you, but at the same time, they are waiting for something like this to occur for whatever reason and unfortunately, for many people, it's a part of life. As much as I wanted to leave, I couldn't. In some way, I felt as if this was karma. I knew was he was a good man. He just came with shit like we all do. I knew he had some type of affection for me. I knew he cared for me as well, but I knew I wasn't *the one* either. I wanted to be *the one*. I wanted to be chosen, and I just wasn't. Again, my mind said one thing, but my heart kept saying something else.

Many of us have a way of doing things that benefit us, not being mindful of how it would affect the other person. As much as the situation took over my heart, I still couldn't leave. I felt angry and betrayed. For some strange reason, it hurt more to leave the situation than to stay.

I allowed myself to go through the hurt and the pain and felt like I just couldn't get back up. Emotionally, I was done. Done fighting for love, done looking for answers. I was tired of having constant questions, like "why me?" and "what did I do?" After several conversations with God, something in me said Tracy, it's still not time for you to leave. The back and forth in my head was causing me to forget things and lose focus daily. In my head I would cuss myself out. In my heart, it was, "I love him." SMH!

There was something we both needed to learn from each other so I stayed. I stayed for another two years, which made it about six years total off and on. As women, many of us don't pay attention to our gut and our heart. Relationships teach us things daily. So, the question I had to ask myself was—how did this situation not only make me *feel*, but how did it *benefit* me?

Situations either make you or break you, your choice. Same as fight or flight. Well this situation did both. How? It broke my heart, self- esteem, interrupted my sleep, things were happening in my body, depression occurred, stress occurred. You name it, it occurred. During the course of the two years, I began to tunnel in on myself.

I had to get right mentally, spiritually, emotionally

and physically. It was at this moment that I realized mental health was important. The struggle to keep it together as a daughter, mom, business owner, and woman seemed impossible at the time. I never lost sight of my faith. I just could not see what God was trying to show me. I prayed and asked God to guide my steps through the process.

First, I had to focus on my health. I did cleanses, I ate differently, I began to meditate more, and I started cleansing and providing my body with the right nutrients. My body needed the right foods, vitamins, and plenty of water.

The second thing I did was focus on my spirituality. In other words, I wanted to get right with The Most High. How do you do that? I spoke to Him more, I prayed more, and I spent quiet time with Him, allowing him to move in my life. I stopped trying to have control of everything. I asked God to walk before my relationship with this person. I would ask Him to show me how to heal my heart, how to mend it. How to forgive someone you love and trust so dearly. I even asked why was it beneficial for me to forgive someone that I hadn't wronged. Don't get me wrong, I had my flaws, but I know I didn't deserve the things that occurred throughout the relationship.

The third thing I focused on was my mental health.

I began feeding my mind the right things. That included reading books, thinking about how I can get my business right, how I can increase my finances, and how I can be the woman I desired to be. I was learning how to create boundaries daily. I listened to different coaches online. I would play music. Basically, anything to get my mind back to where it needed to be. I changed from "*going through* the process to *growing thru* the process." I even changed the way I view others and their situations. I created vision boards, as I had visions in my head of how I wanted my life to be. I also knew having the things I wanted was going to require a certain type of determination.

The relationship was actually showing and teaching me that I had more strength in me than I thought. He taught me to speak up more and he helped me understand what I wanted and no longer wanted in a relationship. He taught me perseverance and consistency because he would open doors for me and walk on the outside of the street while I walked on the inside. And when he held my hand, I felt a sense of security. I felt safe. He taught me how to stay true to myself and never lose sight of that. But the biggest thing he taught me was how to love myself. I realized I loved him more than I loved myself. So, I decided to dig a little deeper to understand why I was not loving myself only to learn it started from not knowing how to love myself. I knew how to love others and I knew how to make others happy, but I didn't know how to do that for me.

It could've started from not having a father figure in my life. The men who I looked up to always had other women. I never saw a male figure treat a woman with love and respect. My dad never played a role in my life. So, therefore, it showed in the types of relationships I had. I always walked with a chip on my shoulder. I always kept a wall up. I always had the attitude that that's not going to be me. It became so hard to deal with. I became super hard on myself because, for a long time, I felt I had to be this beautiful, mean person to get what I wanted.

The last thing was the physical. I had to show up and showing up for me was not just about looking good on the outside. It also consisted of feeling good on the inside. I had to accept my entire self for who I am, to be strong enough to walk away. Once I did, I walked away. Confidently and with my head held high.

Questions for the Reader

1. Have you ever had to walk away from something/
   someone? Describe the experience.

2. How would you have handled this situation if it
   was you?

3. What would be your greatest advice to a friend
   or family member going through a similar
   situation?

4. What steps would you have taken to heal yourself
   after a heartbreak?

CHAPTER 6

Deanen Toney

In Her Peace

Open your eyes wide. Breathe deeply. Inhale—one, two, three, four. Exhale—one, two, three, four. Repeat.

It seemed light-years away from when she became aware. Almost four decades can be a lifetime. Choosing to be responsible for everyone's pleasure was a hell of a load to carry until she realized it was an impossible task.

She was born into a large family—the first grandchild to a single mother of seven and "ghetto siblings" to her grandmother's last two children. She entered a space of constant commotion and a lifestyle of busyness. There was never a dull moment. She often slept with her "sister-aunt," who would butt her head to sleep. The rhythmic motion of the bed was better than a lullaby. As much as she tried fighting sleep for fear of missing something, that ride would knock her out every time.

Being the third toddler in the crowded tenement apartment created space for competition that none of them signed up for. Talk about being a crybaby! If she couldn't be seen in all the goings-on in the house, she damn sure would be heard. Could this be the start of her life's performance? Turns out it was an intolerance to the milk she was drinking. Who knows why it took so long to figure it out or how many "shhhs" her little ears heard before relief came. Somehow, they would know she was there. The absence of lights and cameras never once hindered the show. She decided at an early age to go big or go BIGGER!

The most she could remember about her younger years was that there were always a lot of family gatherings with plenty of food, music, and liquor. She had a ball. Most times, it was fun and exciting. Other times, it was scary but still exciting. When altercations would arise because of the spirits, her little household of four would quickly depart at the lead of her mother, the eldest of the clan of seven. Her mother had been around long enough to see the confusion way before it took place. By the time the first slurred curse word came out, her children had their coats on and were exiting the gathering. No matter whose house or what park they were in, they left and had to hear the gossip of what had taken place after the fact.

She often wondered if her mother was ashamed, wanted no part of the entanglements, or both. She also wondered why her nosey behind craved it so much.

She remembered a very structured home life, calm and consistent weekdays, and exciting weekends with extended family from either side and sometimes both sides together. She loved the togetherness. There were annual birthday celebrations, extraordinary Christmases, family outings to ballparks, circus trips— a host of great memories for the family, the "perfect" family. And then a wrecking ball crashed in on her glass ceiling, leaving deep cuts in her self-image and emotional well-being. She was ten years old when her parents disclosed that her dad, who had been in her life for the past ten years, was not her biological father. This news sent her into a rage that she had never experienced before and ultimately suppressed for the next thirty-five years of her life. It was fire shut up deep inside her innermost parts, and it choked her inner peace.

Once she distanced herself from the cobalt fiery rage that erupted, her first question was, "Is Daddy my sister's dad?" The second question was, "Are we really sisters?"

One "yes" was an instant salve to her wound, which needed constant redressing and recreating to fill the void. The other "yes," hmmm—could it be another doorway to competition? The two sisters, both twins by horoscope but quite different in their approach to life, were a powerful mashup of inseparable yin and yang. No matter what, she knew they had each other.

Too young to care about the streets, she threw herself into her studies, imagination, and creating. She knew she couldn't control much outside of herself, but she could control her grades, her hair, and what she wore. Yes, her parents bought her clothes, but she chose how she put them together. She found her happy place.

As she reflected on middle school and high school, she remembered doing her best while being anxious about her level of achievement. A quiet and competitive student, she set out to prove she was good. She never felt popular among her peers in school or her neighborhood. She never felt *chosen*, only known. She didn't feel desired. That same feeling she felt when she was ten years old. She had to show them she was worth choosing.

In her countless attempts at proving her worth, she found herself people-pleasing at a cost that discounted who she truly was. The young woman who was comfortable in a crowd—showing and proving, performing at multiple levels, trying to be the filler to every void—now found herself feeling exhausted, depleted, and lonely. The energy it took to make them see, hear, and accept her was a price too high to pay for who she was becoming.

Discussions about her biological dad were recurring and continued to extinguish some of the anger she hid inside. After becoming a wife, mother, and entrepreneur, she had to acknowledge and deal with the anger to move forward in her relationships. Suppressing anger once fed her lack of trust. Releasing it has been a catalyst for accepting who she has become and creating peace within.

Finding her peace came at a cost with infinitely rewarding returns. The ripple effect of benefits had added unforeseen value and longevity to her wholeness. She learned how being present could help her move forward strategically. Forgiving and letting go played a role in developing her peace. Saying "no" became an ally when it was once just a thought. Creating while living in peace has supported her flow and ease—forces of their own. There was a time when she created out of desperation and fear, which led to results that she did not want.

After becoming a widow recently, she has decided to accept what exists, embrace it, and be prepared for an opportunity—a gateway of escape. She commits to being pliable and fluid enough to pass through the opening. Fighting it may cause her to become brittle while hardening the scar tissue, making it difficult to transition. She needed to maintain trust and patience in order to remain steadfast and unmovable. To her, it's not about moving from *where* she is but moving from *who* she is. Her core values remain intact while she flows. At the appropriate time, within ebb and flow, she will slip into the opportunity that calls her, and a new creation will form.

One of her recent creations came together in an adventure on her second trip to Africa. Oh, indeed—peace is more than a notion or state in theory. It has been a way of *being*, a choice when things around her were out of her control. Her peace was a great support in dealing with all the details connected to arriving in Ghana.

She had to trust that finances would be available to meet the payment plan, pay the expense of vaccines and visas for three (her two daughters traveled with the group), and have funds for airfare and spending money. Several times, she questioned if she had bitten off more than she could chew. However, the doubts were always superseded by faith and affirming, "I have everything I need." So many magical things occurred to bring the trip to fruition—things that strengthened her faith, deepened her relationships, and widened her scope of resources.

One extraordinary series of events occurred when she got a call from a Jet Blue Airlines employee telling her they were holding her daughter's passport at their gate in Boston. *What?!* First, she had no idea that it wasn't in her possession. Second, she and her girls were in New Orleans visiting family for Thanksgiving. It was the Wednesday morning before Turkey Day, and they needed to fly back to New York to leave for Ghana on Friday. Had they come this far to face misfortune?

Originally, the agent offered to ship the passport to their home, which would not arrive until Monday due to the holiday. *MONDAY?!* That was a no-no. It just wouldn't do. When she took a deep breath and explained their busy itinerary, the agent expressed that using FedEx was their protocol, and she couldn't authorize any other options. However, with a bit of compassion, the agent promised to call her back after speaking with her supervisor.

She paced, took several deep breaths, and prayed in gratitude for a favorable resolution. It's amazing how eighteen minutes could feel like an eternity. That was how long it took for the agent to call back with great news! The airline had a return flight to New Orleans on

Thanksgiving morning and would be carrying the passport. She was given the name of the baggage manager who would have the package and the carousel where she could meet him. The joy and relief that exploded in her were as intense as removing a faja after a long day of work. *Whew, chile!*

Her experience in Ghana was rich, colorful, and alive. Relishing in all the activity made her think with gratitude, *I am here.* Sharing the trip with her family and her community of sisters made it even more special. Despite some irritation and disappointment, she embraced the goodness of the journey. She discovered that such is the nature of most things, so she continued to practice the power of choice and the gift of being in peace. On one of the excursions, the tour guide talked about the beauty and unity of diversity that is found in the print of a native fabric known as Kente cloth. The image reminded her of the beauty of our existence, humanity, and all that is creation. The similarities and the differences—they all have a stake in the beauty of life.

As for the pain and anger that the history of the coast of Ghana stirred within her, she had to dig inside of herself to break up what did not serve her. She embraced moments of gratitude for her tutor, the Serenity Prayer, and her favorite phrase, "passing every ailing concern elsewhere," also known to some as, "casting every care." Acceptance and surrender to evolving in her peace elevated her walk, glow, and freedom.

In her peace, she found that being alone is different from feeling lonely. She was good company—damn good company. She had plenty of practice pleasing people and she was considered "people" too, so let the pleasing begin. She committed to experiencing how loving, exciting, creative, cool, and fun she was becoming. Although she still enjoyed sharing space with others, her peace was a whole vibe.

She discovered that peace is not born out of the absence of conflict. She spent a lot of time searching outside of herself for peace. She looked for it in a lot of places and discovered she didn't need to *find* peace. She had to *receive* peace. The peace that surpasses all understanding was gifted within her and was who she had become.

Questions for the Reader

1. Can you identify some areas in the story where she could have experienced inner conflict? If so, where?

2. In what ways do you experience inner peace?

3. Seek to explore what things and or feelings disrupt your inner peace. What shows up?

4. Is there a particular environment that supports you in connecting within? Picture it and describe it in as much detail as you can.

5. What is your interpretation of the Serenity Prayer?

CHAPTER 7

"Lunas" Tia Carter

First Love: My Gratitude Story

I sit spinning in my not-so-successful leap. Typically, my life has been nothing but constant leaps of faith, and yes, I have landed, but not always on my feet. I am Tia aka Lunas aka Dimples. Let's talk about that real thang. That sweet thang. That *oh my goodness* thang. That God thang!

From the first time I saw His grace, His peace, and His love, I knew I needed the feeling in my life. I was an eight-year-old girl who wanted peace, grace, and love. I had fallen in love with the beauty of God. On one particular Sunday, I ran home to tell my mom I wanted to be a nun and I wanted to marry Jesus. I wanted to serve and be in the bliss of his grace and love. I was told I knew nothing of what I said, and I didn't understand. After all, I was a child.

From that moment on, my life had been full of peaks and valleys. All things were lessons with reasons throughout the seasons. And when I say valleys, I mean the bottom. So low, I contemplated my life and my purpose. Only then would I muster up the strength to push through. I rose to the peak, graduating from college with multiple degrees and beautiful kids along the way. Then I descended time and time again, like a rollercoaster with no stoppage.

As days, weeks, months, and years passed, I stopped questioning and started answering and listening to the soft voices providing me direction and support. Yes, my God speaks to me. My God and the universe place me in front of and connect me to people, places, and things without me having a clue. Now that is some dope shit!

One dope thing God did was align me with two groups of ladies who have been an integral part of my journey. One group was my beginning, and the second group is my middle. My God, what do you have in store? I am an object that must be moved by vibration and energy, and these women are sonic booms!

I was an object that needed to be moved by vibration and energy, and God and the universe were responsible for that movement. I have experienced inspiration, support, healing, direction, love, and spirituality. Now tell me my God is not divine. Through self-reflection, I have come to realize who I am and what I am becoming. As I embraced my purpose of planting seeds of hope, wonder, and greatness and serving others, I discovered my many talents and skills. I am a teacher, mother, philosopher, engineer, physicist, mathematician, gardener, fisherman, seamstress, mason, and herbalist, becoming all things to serve and bring light to many. For the first time in my life, I see my purpose. I am in love, and I have love.

I hold gratitude and gratefulness to my God who tested me, who loves me, and who has always been there for me. My purpose and design were to plant the seeds of hope and ideas and to project/reflect for others. I have realized in these moments that I am a servant of God, and through the days and years, I will have joy, sadness, despair, riches, and poverty. My journey started with one and now I am down to a few.

I remain confident that I will see the goodness of the Lord in the land of the living. It's relatively easy to lift our hands in worship when everything is fine. But it's even more meaningful to God when we can worship Him right smack-dab in the middle of life's challenges.

As I reflected on my journey, I can't help but feel overwhelmed with gratitude. From the moment I fell in love with God as a child, I knew I wanted to serve Him and be in the bliss of His grace and love. Despite facing countless valleys and challenges, I never lost faith and continued to push through, relying on the soft voices that provided direction and support.

As I conclude my reflection, I lift my hands in worship, knowing that my gratitude and love for God will continue to guide my path and bring peace and joy.

* * * * *

As I look forward to my future and what it holds in possibilities and expectations, a story of gratitude emerges that highlights Gratitude in Action. It is about a woman who discovers a mysterious object on her morning walk. As Sarah walked down the quiet street, she couldn't help but notice the odd object sitting on the sidewalk. It was a small, metallic box with intricate patterns etched into the sides. She'd never seen anything like it before.

Curiosity getting the better of her, Sarah approached the box and picked it up. It was surprisingly heavy, and she could feel a faint vibration emanating from it. She turned it over in her hands, searching for any clues as to what it could be.

She put the box in her bag and headed home. Greeted by the tasks of the evening, she tossed her bag in the corner and settled down for the day.

Sarah's days, nights, and weeks passed with no thought of the box. Then one day, she received a call from a college friend sharing the news of her illness. Like any friend, Sarah was saddened by the news and sought solace through prayer. To relieve stress, she began tidying up the house. As she does so, she stumbles across the bag. She opened it and pulled out the box. *What a nice-looking box*, she thought to herself as she placed it on the mantle over the fireplace.

The next day, Sarah received a text from her friend asking if she would come for a visit. Sarah's first thought was, "What can I do to cheer her up?" Immediately, the box came to mind. Without hesitation, she grabbed the box and went to her friend's home. Excited to see each other, they embraced and the box fell to the ground. What they saw inside was amazing. It was a tiny, glowing crystal pulsing with energy. Puzzled by this unique object, they both sat in silence. Sarah stared at the crystal, knowing there was something special about it. That's when she noticed her friend's face, full of light and glow.

In amazement, Sarah screamed, "My God!" Full of fear, her friend asked, "What Sarah?" Sarah pointed to her friend's face. "Your face! It looks different!" The friend looked at her face in a nearby mirror and was surprised. "So," Sarah asked, "how do you feel?"

"I feel amazing!"

Sarah knew she could not keep the crystal hidden with all its glory. So, she gifted the box to her friend and kept the crystal. She researched its properties and discovered that it had incredible healing powers. She decided to use the crystal to help people.

She set up a clinic and began to treat patients, using the crystal to cure everything from cancer to broken bones. The news spread quickly, and soon people were coming from all over to see Sarah and the miraculous crystal. She became a legend, known for her incredible healing powers.

Years later, Sarah passed away, but her legacy lived on. The crystal was passed down from generation to generation, each healer using it to help those in need.

Sarah's name became synonymous with compassion and healing, a testament to the power of one person to make a difference. Hence, gratitude in action.

Questions for the Reader

1. How has God's grace shown up in your life?

2. What are you grateful for?

3. In what way(s) does Sarah's story resonate with you?

CHAPTER 8

Suzanne Castro

Love and Reiki

Dedicated to Ana Aleyka Dominguez—my friend, my sister, my niece, my everything. I love you with all my heart and soul. Thank you for loving me unconditionally. Namaste.

Love saved my life.

I was spiraling deep into a rabbit hole—hurting, lost, violent, and traumatized. I was drinking so much for many years to numb it all, losing my way. I was scrolling on social media with no interest, no love in my heart, no true happiness, *or so I thought*—just masks and lies so others couldn't see the true shit I was in. I couldn't see the love right next to me and all around me. I was at the point of losing it all, asking God to give me some type of sign. I was angry, always ready to fly off the handle.

While online, I came across a Reiki Master explaining the practice—how it's a universal life energy that we all have and how we must heal ourselves first. It sparked a light in me to want more, to want to feel something deep again.

So, my journey began. I found Suzanne again. I also found a man who truly loves me unconditionally. We met when I was at my lowest. It was a time in my life when I didn't care about anything or anyone, including myself. I had a different mask on every day, plus the physical illness I had going on. The chronic stomach pain of not eating for days on end. From the outside, I had a lot going for myself. I had a great job at the hospital for over twenty years, three beautiful daughters, and was a new grandma. My days and nights were spent having dinner dates, partying, and drinking. It was all a lie—I was lonely, unhappy, scared, and felt invisible. That was until Elliot came along to embrace this fireball, and he never let me go.

It was a long day at the hospital. A few of us were going to dinner for drinks, fake conversations, and fake love interactions. We all decided to continue the party at the local bar and billiards hall. There was a game going on in the back. The music was rocking, and drinks were flowing. I was dancing and putting money in the jukebox, so the music didn't stop. Then, I had to use the restroom. As I passed the pool tables, I felt someone looking as they stood in the corner of the room. I peeked, but quickly looked away and went to the restroom. As I tried to pass the crowd that formed in front of the restroom, I felt someone reach out to grab my arm. I yanked my arm and gave a daring look. The man apologized, and then I walked back over to my group.

As the night went on, I continued to dance. Then, the barmaid came out from behind the bar and handed me a new drink. I told her I didn't order a drink. She then told me the gentleman in the corner sent it to me. I looked over towards the corner. It was the "peek-a-boo" man who had grabbed my arm. Wow, his smile was amazing. I took the drink and gestured a "thank you" to him. Later, I walked over to get a better look at the mystery man—his game was good, and his focus was intense. I started dancing again, then felt someone dancing with me. It was *him*.

He extended his hand to me.

"Hello, my name is Elliot."

"Hi, I'm Suzanne," I said as I shook his hand firmly.

We both smiled and finished our dance. I asked him what brought him out that night since I was amazed how he managed to get to the dance floor so fast when

I just saw him shooting balls. He replied, "I made myself lose, so I can meet you."

We talked and laughed. My fresh-ass grabbed his face and kissed him. It was an impulsive move, but his smile and his lips were inviting. He was just as surprised as I was.

"Did you just…?"

Before he could finish the question, I plopped another juicy one on him!

I started to feel weird. *I don't want to be bothered by any man. I'm in my "hoe phase."*

"Well, I'm leaving tomorrow for Atlanta to visit my daughters. I work half a day then I will be heading to the Chinese Bus Depot downtown, which leaves at 2:30 in the afternoon."

He said, "Okay, I'll take you to the bus."

I looked at him in surprise. "Sure, okay. Right."

Yeah, right. He thinks I believe that shit. Elliot insisted on taking my friend Iaysha and me home from the bar. He dropped us off, and we looked at each other while giggling.

The next day, I was rushing to finish with work and of course, something came up at the last minute in the hospital. After work, I ran to the bus stop and jumped on the bus to the train station. As I sat on the noisy bus, I thought about the fun night I had with that smooth-talking liar with a gorgeous smile. My thoughts were interrupted as I came to my stop in front of the 180th Tremont Avenue Train Station in the Bronx. I was walking towards the station when I heard honking and yelling.

"SUZANNE!" I looked back, and to my surprise, it was *him*—Elliot. I stopped and asked him what he was doing there.

"I told you I would take you to your bus."

"No, it's okay. I still have to pack and take a shower. That's nice of you, but no, thank you."

He jumped out of his car and said, "Please! I'll wait for you and take you to your bus."

He opened the car door, ushered me in, and tried to kiss me. But this time. I wasn't having it. I was sober and embarrassed that I'd kissed him the night before. In my mind, I tried blaming the alcohol. Then, I felt him tap me. He was holding a beautiful bouquet of flowers. Oh boy, he got a kiss then!

We arrived at my place, where I lived with my roommate, Ana. She was my other savior, but that's another story. He waited until I was done getting ready. Then, we headed downtown to the Chinese Bus Depot and arrived before it was time for me to depart. When I tried to secure my bus ticket, I found out that they sold my ticket and rescheduled me for the 8:30 p.m. bus. It was 1:45 p.m. I had no money except what was set aside for spending in Atlanta. I was hungry and crying to this stranger who was just being the kindest, most loving individual I had ever met.

He calmed me down and said, "Listen, I got you. We'll go eat, have a drink, and talk some more. I will wait with you."

Who is this man? What is going on, God?

Elliot looked me in the eyes and said, "Suzanne, you will never ride the bus again. EVER!" (I never rode on a bus again!)

I got on the bus for my fourteen-hour journey. Elliot and I talked on the phone the entire ride to Atlanta. We laughed and got a little closer. We even talked some more during my trip. *Hmm, this feels nice,* I thought. But I was scared and starting to feel weird. So, when I returned home from Atlanta, I tried to self-sabotage. I didn't answer his calls—I hid from him. I began renting a room from a man who turned out to be a rapist and tried to hurt me. During this time, my ex and I were also still having sex. From that moment, I began to spiral downward and eventually, had to be hospitalized. I was in and out of the hospital and a mere one hundred pounds. Everyone would say, "Wow, you look good. OMG, you're so skinny." But the chronic pain and loneliness that I was living with was crazy.

As the months went by, doctors came, and doctors

went. I was still hiding from Elliot. On one of my days of despair, I looked at my phone and saw that Elliot was calling. *He doesn't give up.* I hesitated but eventually declined his call. My living situation was scary then. I was fighting off a man who painted a picture of himself being an awesome landlord. He claimed that he would take care of me. He even introduced me to his girlfriend and family to make me feel comfortable. My stay in the room became weird. My landlord was drinking every weekend, pacing in front of my room while knocking and whispering, telling me to let him in. I would yell, "Go to your room. You're drunk, stop!"

Music blasted from his room every weekend while he got high and drunk until he started pacing in front of my room again. This became his crazy routine. I had nowhere to go. Months went by as I dealt with everything—my living situation, work, and hiding from Elliot. I was living in fear but also, putting myself in awful situations that caused me to risk my life day in and day out with no concern.

One day while at work, I fainted. It was as though my body said, "NO MORE, SUZANNE!" I woke up in the hospital with an IV in both arms and suffering from unbearable pain. There was even a tube coming out of my nose. I was dealing with bowel obstruction— my intestines had turned inside out. I wasn't taking care of myself. I didn't LOVE myself. I had given up on myself but wasn't aware of it. I felt I was dying inside. My hospital stay became even more traumatic. I was so drugged up that I would be in and out of consciousness throughout each day. I woke up one time and found my landlord in my room. He was not letting anyone in because he was "taking care of me." Yuck. My mind started playing games on me. *Did this man see me naked, Lord?* I thanked him and told him to leave. As he walked out, he said, "I'll see you at home." *Oh Lord, help me!*

One day during my stay in the hospital, my friend came to sit with me. As we talked, I showed him my phone and told him about the time I met Elliot. I mentioned that Elliot was still calling me nonstop. My friend and I were joking about him being a stalker.

"Be careful, Sue,'" my friend said to me. I just laughed.

Then, my phone began to ring.

"Look! It's him—Elliot."

My friend told me to answer the phone, but I refused. At that moment, the curtain swung open. It was Elliot.

"Why haven't you answered my calls?" he asked. "I've been so worried."

My friend was about to leave, but I gave him the

look of death. So, he sat back down and looked at Elliot with awe—he knew this man was not playing. I asked Elliot how he knew I was in the hospital, and he told me that he took a chance because his gut told him something was wrong. He called my office and noticed that my coworker was picking up my phone in my absence. He then drove to the hospital where I worked and gave them the name I gave him, Suzanne Castro. My married name was Suzanne Castro-Cole, so they told him they couldn't find anyone by that name. One of the old security guards who knew me approached him and asked him how he could help since Elliot looked upset.

"Oh yes, my girl, Suzy," the security guard replied as he gave Elliot my room number. "Room 1055, bed A."

So, the man finds me again. Elliot reached out, grabbed my hand, and asked, "Why Suzy?"

"I didn't want you to see me like this."

"You look beautiful!"

I got tubes coming out of everywhere and I look beautiful to him—WHAT?! The anger and confusion from my past hurt hit me hard, so I asked him to leave. As he was walking out, my ex was coming in. These two men had never met or seen each other.

Elliot turned to him, tapped him hard on the chest,

and said, "What's up man?"

My ex was startled and looked at him with confusion, then anger. Elliot winked at me and left. My ex was very upset and asked, "Who the hell was that?"

I answered, "My friend, and you can get out too!"

My discharge day arrived after being in the hospital for four days. I left silently in a cab and went back to my room—lonely and afraid of what I would have to fight off. My two older brothers came by to visit. I told them about the creep I lived with. They were upset at me and my situation because I was putting myself in danger. Yes, I knew it, but didn't care at the time.

I went back to my same daily routine—work, mask the pain, play, and repeat. Elliot would call me, and we would talk for hours. I told him where I lived and who I lived with. He didn't like it either, but *who cares?*

I ignored all the signs. It had been months, and Elliot and I were talking more frequently on the phone. Elliot told me how close he lived and would invite me to come over. But my answer was always no. One weekend, I was coming out of my building and saw Elliot parked in front, waiting for me. I was startled by him being there. He told me he came to bring me something, but I never gave him the apartment number. I informed him that my landlord said I couldn't have visitors unless it was my brothers. Elliot didn't like that either. Again, *who cares?*

Excitedly, Elliot proceeded to show me what he had for me—chips, soda, juice, and candy. He wasn't sure which ones I liked, so he bought them all. I looked at him and told him I didn't want any of it. As he looked back in shock, he asked me where I was headed.

"I'm going to lunch at my favorite local Dominican restaurant," I answered with an attitude. "Bye."

Elliot replied with a smile, "Bye? I'm hungry too, so I'll go with you."

When he smiled, I felt a little something inside, so I allowed him to join me. We had an awesome time talking and laughing. After he paid for our meals, we slowly walked back to my building and talked along the way. It was nice. When we got to my place, I thanked him, and we said our goodbyes. I felt him watching me through the glass door until my elevator came. He smiled, winked, then left. *God, what is happening?*

A few days later, Elliot called me at work and asked me to go to Willie Steakhouse for dinner. I tried not to go. I said I was meeting my daughter, but he told me to bring her along. *Oh, Lord. He doesn't know what he's doing inviting my greedy daughter to dinner.* When my daughter arrived at the restaurant, I introduced the two, and they hit it off right away. It upset me that he was befriending my child. I thought to myself, *I don't want happiness, togetherness, friendship, and love from this man.* I felt the sabotage monster trying to creep in again. I went back to hiding and ignored Elliot again.

A few days later, my daughter met me after work to head to the supermarket. While shopping, I kept losing her in the aisles. I finally caught up to her and noticed she was whispering and trying to talk on her phone. I heard her say my name, so I asked her who she was talking to.

"It's Elliot, Mom," she replied. "He's been calling you. You're not answering him?"

Oh, Lord. I lost it in the supermarket. I grabbed her phone and told him to never call her again. Then, I turned to my daughter and ripped her a new one for exchanging numbers with him.

When we left and went back to my place, my creepy landlord was upstairs. He lost his mind when he saw my daughter and began complimenting her beauty to me. I thanked him, trying to brush him off by ignoring his comments. As my daughter and I ate dinner, the creep stood in front of my door, talking through it to ask if my daughter needed anything. We both answered him with a hard rejection. My daughter was very upset with my living situation. I calmed her down, but she left and told the creep that she would be visiting again. He got excited, but she meant it in a way of taking care of me.

Time continued to pass. I was juggling a so-called friendship with my ex, a friendship with Elliot, my job, fake friendships, not feeling well, toxicity, anger, and loneliness. I was exhausted, so I shut down. But Elliot continued to reach out. I tried to ignore him, but it was getting difficult. However, I refused to give in to him.

I'm missing something here. Why am I so sad and angry? I feel so lost. I kept seeing commercials about love on television, online, and on billboards, all around me. I was seeing different people speaking about healing and loving yourself. I tried to begin my healing journey by taking small steps like answering some of Elliot's calls here and there. We started to get closer. But again, I felt weird and confused. So, I reached out to Ana who I looked at as a niece, sister, friend, everything. I updated her on all my shit.

She started joking by saying in Spanish, "Suzy ese tu mariiooo!" which meant, "Girl, that's your MAN—stop playing!" I got so angry and upset with her for saying those words to me. But then, she told me he loves me.

Elliot and I were becoming closer as friends but from a distance. He would pick me up from work and take me home. Some days, we would sit in the car and talk or go out to eat. At the end of our evenings, I would give him a little smooch and bid him a good night. We would talk on the phone all night until one of us fell asleep. *Wow, this feels nice. Is he being for real? Can't be.*

As time went on, Elliot and Ana became very close friends. They would call each other, have dinner, and he would even confess his love for me to Ana. I started feeling weird again. He told Ana that I stopped answering his calls and responding to his messages. Afterward, Ana called me and yelled, "Sue, you know, ESE TU MARIIOOOO!" I wanted to kill her, but we laughed until we couldn't laugh anymore. I promised Ana that I would speak to him and make plans to see him again. It felt surreal having a man want me so bad that he would try anything not to lose me, so I called him. *My heart was racing. Why?*

"Hello, how are you?"

"Hi," he responded. "Man, I'm so happy you called. I'm so happy to hear your voice. Why do you do this to me? I called Ana because I didn't want to just show up to your job again. You weren't so happy when I did that before."

"No, I wasn't," I replied. "And yes, I know you called Ana. What the hell, Elliot? What is your problem? Why do you keep on? You just don't get it!"

"No, the one who doesn't get it is you, Suzanne,"

he said. "I will not stop. What are you doing tonight? Can I see you?"

I told him I needed to go grocery shopping. So, he offered to come with me and help carry my bags.

"Please, I want to see you," Elliot begged.

Elliot met me at my local supermarket and helped me shop. He acted so silly, telling everyone that I was his wife just so the local men who saw me daily would know I belonged to him. As he helped me bring my groceries inside, I stopped him at the elevator.

"You don't want me to see you to your door?" he asked.

"Well, the landlord doesn't want another man besides my brothers to come in," I replied.

"Are you crazy? You pay rent, right?"

"$650.00 a month."

"So, I can come in!"

We laughed and he came in to help me put away the groceries. I showed him my room, and we got a quickie in, which helped me get rid of some pent-up shit that I was causing. We finished, washed up, and laughed like two sneaky kids.

We were in the kitchen getting some water when the door of the apartment opened. It was Willie, the landlord. He came in and extended his hand, asking if Elliot was another family member. Elliot told him he was my boyfriend. Willie laughed and told him that I had no boyfriend. Then, he went to his room and closed the door. We looked at each other and laughed. Later that evening, we took a ride and had a good talk. Elliot told me I was the only person for him. I took the opportunity to explain all my insecurities. He also shared his insecurities and fears. We connected. Hours passed, and he drove me back home.

When I got to my door, I tried to open it, but my key wouldn't work. I tried it again and realized that Willie put a padlock on the door while I was out. *Oh my God!* As I called Elliot to let him know what happened, Willie opened his door.

"Oh, I thought you were staying with him because he's your boyfriend, right?"

I cursed his ass out and went to bed. I knew he was drunk when he started knocking on my door, asking for me to forgive him. I called my brothers, and they came the next day to have a word with him. They threatened his life, setting him straight. While all this was happening, Elliot was also very upset. He came over and had a few words with Willie too.

"Fuck you, you fucking Puerto Rican!" Willie yelled at Elliot.

The police had to get in the middle of all this, so I left with Elliot. He wanted me to move in with him because I was risking my life living with Willie and his constant drinking and intimidating behavior. I had nowhere else to go. I was homeless *again*. So, I went to Elliot's house, crying and asking God why was this happening to me.

Elliot was running around trying to make me comfortable in his home. It was the weekend, so I spent some quality time with him and his dog, Kernel. Although my friendship was growing with Elliot, I still had doubts about the decision to live with him. *What is happening? I don't even know this man. How can I move in so soon? Where am I going to go?* We agreed that we would try it out and if it didn't work out, he would help me find a place. He would even pay the rent for a few months until I could handle it. So, we gave it a try.

On that Monday morning, Elliot drove me to work, brought me to lunch, and then, picked me up to take me to my old building so I could pick up some things. While there, I spoke with Willie and told him I was moving out. He wanted to talk about things, but there was nothing to talk about. It went too far. When Elliot and I made it back downstairs in front of the building, Willie drove up and told me to come to his car so he could speak to me. As I leaned over his driver-side window, he asked me why I was leaving the building. But then, he saw Elliot and lost his mind.

"You're leaving for this fucking Puerto Rican?" Willie yelled.

I moved away from the car. Willie thrust the car in reverse and jammed on the gas pedal hard to run me and Elliot over. We jumped on the curb, and then he backed up and tried again. It was crazy. He then whipped out a knife and said he was going to cut us up. I needed a police escort to move my things after that.

What saved me was having it all recorded so I was able to press charges. To make matters worse for Willie, the court added rape to his charges because he assaulted a girl when I first moved into the building. All I could think about during this time was that Elliot and his persistent love saved my life. Despite all this love, I still felt weird, unhappy, confused, and fearful. I was so scared.

One night at home with Elliot, I was scrolling on social media and found a Reiki Master on TikTok. So, I researched Reiki and then reached out to her. I loved what I had learned about the practice. It's never too late to learn about love. I gave in to the feelings, the vibrations, the vulnerability, the security, the joy, and the fulfillment I was feeling in my heart. The love I was feeling within. That entire time, I didn't realize that the "weird feeling" I had was *love*. There was a sense of trust I now had within me. I learned to give in to the faith within my heart, the faith in God, and LOVE.

I am so grateful for the love and patience within Elliot. In our nine years together, this man has never ceased to amaze me. One time, he surprised me with a trip to Vegas a week before my birthday.

He said, "Sue, let's go to Vegas!"

"Yes!" I responded.

He got us a beautiful room at the Luxor Hotel. As I unpacked, he came up behind me to hug and kiss me. Then, he said four words I will never forget.

"Sue, let's get married."

I looked at him and laughed. But he didn't laugh with me.

"You serious?" I asked.

"Yes," he said.

Oh, what a nice night of love and lovemaking we had. We even had room service, so there was a beautiful fruit salad, burgers, fries, chocolates, and LOVE. I was awakened the next morning with more kisses. Elliot yanked the drapes open and moved around the room acting excited and giddy. When I asked him what was going on, he told me to get up because we had a lot to do that day. We enjoyed a great breakfast, then went off to downtown Las Vegas. When we got to the marriage license bureau, we were the fourth couple there. I heard the clerk behind the window telling the other couples they had to have an appointment plus the fee to be paid in advance.

"Damn Sue, we are not prepared," he said.

I replied, "It's okay, Papi. Let's go have fun and we'll do it another time."

Elliot suggested that we go to the window anyway just to be sure.

"Hello, you gorgeous couple," the clerk said. "So, we are getting married, huh?"

I tried to tell her we weren't getting married, but Elliot told her we were. I looked at him with shock as he whipped out all the receipts of payment, our appointment that we were on time for, and all the necessary documents. We both laughed and hugged.

I whispered in his ear, "I'm punishing you when we get back to the hotel room."

"You promise?" he asked as we continued to laugh with excitement.

When we returned, he had a beautiful night planned for us with a show and dinner. *Wow. So, this is LOVE, huh?* The next morning, we felt the excitement of our wedding day—we were happily in love, giggly in love, vulnerable in love, honestly in love, transparently in love, and *in* love *with* love. I continued to rest and asked no questions—he had it all under control.

After we showered, we headed to a crystal mystical

shop in the hotel, then we took a nice ride downtown to go sightseeing. We approached a tall building and then walked in.

"Hello, do you have an appointment?" asked the security guard.

Elliot answered with a smile, "Yes."

Then, I started to laugh. "Of course, you do."

The laughter stopped abruptly when the security guard asked, "Do you have a witness?"

We looked at each other, then looked around and told him we didn't have one. He informed us that we had ten minutes to find a witness, or we would lose our spot. We would then have to make another appointment. That wasn't an option since we were scheduled to fly out the next day. So, we went outside and saw a meter man giving someone a ticket. Elliot asked him if he could do us a favor and be a witness to our marriage.

He looked so surprised, but said, "Yes, I would LOVE to!" With excitement in his voice, he called his wife to tell her the news. We celebrated a little and ran back to the building.

Our celebration came to a halt when the security guard said, "He can't be your witness. He works for the county of Nevada!"

The meter man said, "I don't work for the county

of Nevada. We are a private company!"

The security guard still refused.

With frustration, Elliot replied, "Hey, who is your supervisor? I want him or her on the phone! NOW! You're not putting a damper on my special day, fukouttaheaaaa!"

The security guard got her supervisor on the phone and to our amazement, they approved our witness. We went off to the second floor to be married. The wedding officiant's name was Randi, like my oldest daughter. *This was destiny!*

We were officially married! It was all such a fun and loving experience with my new husband. He cried and laughed as he had his vows in his pocket, shaking as he read them. I knew I loved that man.

I thank God for allowing me to connect back to Him and the power of love. I am thankful for the universal life force energy, known as Reiki. *I am love. I am Reiki.*

Because of Reiki, I was able to dive deep into myself. I have explored ways to shape myself for my greatest manifestation, connecting with the loving kindness within and the loving kindness around me. I express gratitude for this sacred moment of love with a smile in my heart. Happiness is the vein that takes root and grows within the heart, never outside of it. It works from my inside out as I am becoming a powerful creator. I have learned to love myself so I can call upon the love I so desire because love is my greatest power. Reaching in deep and allowing love to flow has brought an abundance in all areas of my life while also using the power of gratitude. Thanks for walking together with me through this pathway of love, unconditional love. May we all be happy in love and free.

SueWoo loves you!

Questions for the Reader

1. When was a time you felt loved deeply, and who was it from?

2. Can you remember who made your heart flutter with excitement and love? Where were you when you met them?

CHAPTER 9

Paula Lambkin

Abundance

D r. Ena Tychus defines abundance as "Having a superfluous supply of something, whatever your something is, so much so, that this something can overflow into another life or community and make impact."

Abundance is such an overarching theme, and it's something with which I've been grappling. I've been trying to piece together various aspects of my life, from moments of laughter and healing to the abundance of relationships and friendships that have shaped me. Despite lacking female role models after my mother passed away, I found solace in a lifelong friend who became like a second mother to me, filling the void of guidance. As I reflect on my past, I realize that while I've had abundance in certain areas, I've also faced challenges, particularly in terms of lacking guidance and struggling to find my purpose. Despite these struggles, I've tried to excel in various roles, including nursing and relationships, although I often felt like I was just going through the motions without a clear direction.

My journey has been one of self-discovery and healing, and while I never imagined myself writing a book, I've come to realize the importance of sharing my story. However, revisiting painful memories and confronting the past has been daunting, and I've questioned my strength to do so. Yet, amidst these doubts, I've found strength in my faith and in the support of those around me. My career as a nurse has been a source of fulfillment, and I've come to see it as a form of missionary work, guided by a higher power. Even though I often lacked versions of guidance in the way I may have wanted or needed it, my life's career is providing support and care for others. I find myself being in positions to "fill in the gap" for those who may be lacking in a way that I'm now able to provide. To do so is, in itself, a blessing.

Looking ahead, I'm preparing to embrace my story and move forward with clarity and purpose. Despite the challenges I've faced, I have the resilience and determination to overcome them. I'm grateful for the abundance of blessings in my life and for the powerful people who have supported me along the way. As I embark on this next chapter, I'm filled with optimism and a renewed sense of purpose. I'm ready to share more of my story and to continue striving towards my goals, knowing that I am supported by faith and surrounded by abundance.

Questions for the Reader

1. At the beginning of this chapter, I shared Dr. Tychus' definition of abundance. What's your definition of abundance?

2. How much of your definition is based on the past or past beliefs?

3. What are your top 3 experiences that make you feel abundant (and apply them)?

CHAPTER 10

Vallori Thomas

The Whole Nine

O n behalf of each of the authors who've shared their stories in this collective, thank you for journeying with us. Our hope is that our stories spark a *fresh* perspective, and you discover a new possibility you hadn't considered in the "way" you view the challenges that have shaped you in this moment. What I know for sure is that we are far more resilient than we might allow ourselves to think or believe. It's perspective and practices I call "Possibilitology." What Is Possibilitology? It begins with possibility thinking (PT), a mindset that engages in the exploration of possibility. It allows you to engage in transforming what is, into what might be.

My team and I have created a number of resources to support and empower you in the practice of possibility thinking. Put the maximum impact of PT to work in your life by enrolling in one of our in-person workshops or eLearning courses. Subscribe to our newsletter. Travel to an exotic destination with us to make a difference on one of our purpose-centered tours.

Maybe you would like to add *Possibilitology, It's A Great Day To Be Amazing* to your personal library or surround yourself with daily upward messaging from the *Wholeheartedly* team by following us on Instagram and Facebook. Our intent is that you experience every day…wholeheartedly!

With Love,
Vallori Thomas
www.ValloriThomas.com

Meet The Authors

TAUNDREA TAVADA has had her fair share of

life "life-ing" along her journey as a
mechanical engineer working in
construction. She attended Tuskegee
University, is a licensed life coach,
and seen as "the ultimate personal
assistant." Taundrea helps clients see
themselves so they can ultimately choose themselves.
She currently resides in Georgia.

EVELYN WHITE was born in the Bronx, NY. At
the age of five, separated from her
siblings, Evelyn went to live with
her grandparents, who later moved
to South Carolina. Ultimately,
Evelyn ended back up in New
York and went on to serve,
supervise, and organize as Union

Rep/Shop Steward and as a mail carrier at the United
States Post Office for twenty-seven years. As a mother of
two and grandmother to one, Evelyn is living out her
purpose, focusing on being the example she wants to see

in the world, and her community.

ANA MONCION DOMINGUEZ was born in
Santo Domingo, Dominican
Republic in 1966. She
migrated to New York in 1968
and settled in the Bronx, where
she currently resides. Ana
attended the High School of
Music and Arts and New York
City Technical College. She was married in 1985 and
gave birth to the love of her life, Akeyla, in 1986.

KIMBERLY GIVENS is a twenty-year beauty
 industry expert, certified life
coach, motivational and
awareness speaker, author
(*Strategies to K.I.M.*), and
graduate of the University
of Maryland Eastern. She has combined her talents as
a gifted business owner and stylist with her love for
empowering women. As such, her goal is to help them
create spaces to find the forgiveness to let go and allow
themselves grace to set intentions to keep it moving.

TRACIA WALTERS was born on the wonderful

island of Barbados as the youngest of eight children. The mother of four is the founder and owner of Luxurious Seduction LLC, where she assists women in looking and feeling beautiful. She is an ICF-certified coach and helps people birth their power from within. Through coaching, she was able to launch Power, Purpose, & Renewal LLC.

DEANEN TONEY is the founder of Toney Beauty Network, a development agency where people are their highest asset, and enhancing life is a priority. Leading the enterprise for twenty-three years is Beauty In You, a rejuvenating salon experience. To date, the company has

expanded operations in business coaching, spiritual ministry, and financial services.

"LUNAS" TIA CARTER was born in Baltimore,

Maryland, to a spicy five-foot woman from the South and a six-foot hippie father from the North. A mother, wife, sister, friend, and businesswoman, Tia grew up in the humble inner city of Baltimore and graduated from Tuskegee University with a bachelor's degree in electrical engineering and a Bachelor of Science in Physics. She became an integral part of a global corporate company in product development and an entrepreneur with small business ventures in intellectual property and real estate & agriculture.

SUZANNE CASTRO was born and raised in New

York City. The mother of three beautiful daughters and five grandchildren is a certified Reiki instructor specializing in sound healing. She has learned how to give love and how to receive love and spread it *wholeheartedly*.

PAULA LAMBKIN is a registered nurse of thirty-eight years and a graduate of Hampton University. Born in Passaic, New Jersey, her most memorable nursing moments were working with Planned Parenthood, advocating for women's rights. Inspired to provide warmth and hope to her  patients and families, healing with laughter is her ministry and goal. She is an avid traveler and loves to explore international culture, cuisine, and the heart of the community.

VALLORI THOMAS is an accredited member of the Forbes Coaches Council, an ICF-Certified Coach, 2021 WeInspire Movement for Change Ambassador, and the Founder of The Institute at WOW Coaching and Consulting. She is the author  of *POSSIBILITOLOGY: It's A Great Day To Be Amazing*, and co-author of *Through It All We're Still Standing*.

Known for delivering potent results, a practitioner of context mastery, Vallori is adept at vision-building and breakthrough learning. Her field of expertise is professional development, DEIB, leadership optimization, and corporate culture & team dynamics. She is an enthusiastic and indefatigable keynote speaker and facilitator who has delivered empowerment training for WOCC for Harvard University Graduate Students, as well as adult and youth leadership programs in New York, Los Angeles, Washington, D.C., Seattle, South Carolina, and Atlanta.